Piano

Jules MOUQUET

La Flûte de Pan

(Op. 15)

Concerto/Sonata for Flute and Orchestra/Piano

Edited by
SIR JAMES GALWAY

CONTENTS

Southern
MUSIC

La Flûte de Pan by Jules Mouquet
Performance notes

When approaching this piece, the first problem is to find a tempo which suits you in the first and third movements. I think the metronome marks are too quick as suggested by the composer or his editor. In the first movement, I play the half note at 72. In the second movement, I play at the recommended tempi. In the last and most difficult movement I play dotted quarter note at 95. The breathing is most difficult in the first and third movements.

I. Pan and the Shepherds
I pay particular attention to the dynamics in this movement. For example, the first four bars of the flute part are *piano* followed by *mezzo forte* for the next four bars. The reason we pay so much attention to the dynamics is that we want to be able to build to a good, strong, vibrant *forte* at measure 19. From this point, keep the tempo. At measure 39, it is most important to play softly, the reason being that it requires good breath control and we want to preserve the breath in order to play uninterrupted to measure 49. Here, the breathing is most important. I have marked little breaths in the part (✓), and you really have to take them to survive. As there is not a lot of time to take a breath, I would recommend that you don't open your mouth so much but that you acquire the technique of taking a lot of breath through your lips in the embouchure position. At measure 113, pay close attention to the markings, as it's only *forte*, and "*con brio*". It is not a bad idea to practice in three octaves the scales of F major and D minor. Here and there, I have inserted a slur, or changed the articulation for the better.

II. Pan and the Birds
Here we want to get a very good, soft mood going: *pianissimo*, *leggiero*, and a soft articulation. A soft touch on the keys will also help greatly. At measure 17, begin to liven up the tempo by pushing ahead ever so slightly. There are a lot of crescendos in this piece and I would advise not to get too loud too quickly. Here I have inserted some dynamic markings to help you with this. In measure 21 when you return to the *tempo primo*, make sure you get to the right tempo. Don't play slower simply because you've got a beautiful melody to play. Be careful not to accent the first note after the bar line. At measure 53, don't force the tone but use your most beautiful singing and projecting sound.

III. Pan and the Nymphs
This is the most demanding and difficult of all the three movements. When you see a crescendo, don't begin straight away to get loud, but delay the crescendo. I would recommend that you practice your chromatic scales as this will help you play most of this piece. The passage between measures 24-47 can be more successful if you don't try to play too loud. *Staccato*, especially in the low notes, is more successful when you play soft.

I hope you enjoy playing this piece and working on it as much as I have done in the past.

Sir James Galway
Switzerland, 2017

La Flûte de Pan

Concerto/Sonata for Flute and Orchestra/Piano

I. Pan et les bergers

I. Pan and the Shepherds

Piano

Jules Mouquet, Op. 15

O Pan qui habites la montagne, change nous
de tes douces lèvres une chanson, change nous
la en t'accompagnant du Roseau pastoral.

(Alcée)

Piano

II. Pan et les oiseaux
II. Pan and the Birds

Assis à l'ombre de ce bois solitaire
ô Pan, pourquoi tires tu de ta flûte ces
sons délicieux?

(Anyté)

Jules MOUQUET

La Flûte de Pan

(Op. 15)

Concerto/Sonata for Flute and Orchestra/Piano

Edited by
SIR JAMES GALWAY

CONTENTS

La Flûte de Pan by Jules Mouquet
Performance notes

When approaching this piece, the first problem is to find a tempo which suits you in the first and third movements. I think the metronome marks are too quick as suggested by the composer or his editor. In the first movement, I play the half note at 72. In the second movement, I play at the recommended tempi. In the last and most difficult movement I play dotted quarter note at 95. The breathing is most difficult in the first and third movements.

I. Pan and the Shepherds
I pay particular attention to the dynamics in this movement. For example, the first four bars of the flute part are *piano* followed by *mezzo forte* for the next four bars. The reason we pay so much attention to the dynamics is that we want to be able to build to a good, strong, vibrant *forte* at measure 19. From this point, keep the tempo. At measure 39, it is most important to play softly, the reason being that it requires good breath control and we want to preserve the breath in order to play uninterrupted to measure 49. Here, the breathing is most important. I have marked little breaths in the part (✓), and you really have to take them to survive. As there is not a lot of time to take a breath, I would recommend that you don't open your mouth so much but that you acquire the technique of taking a lot of breath through your lips in the embouchure position. At measure 113, pay close attention to the markings, as it's only *forte*, and "*con brio*". It is not a bad idea to practice in three octaves the scales of F major and D minor. Here and there, I have inserted a slur, or changed the articulation for the better.

II. Pan and the Birds
Here we want to get a very good, soft mood going: *pianissimo*, *leggiero*, and a soft articulation. A soft touch on the keys will also help greatly. At measure 17, begin to liven up the tempo by pushing ahead ever so slightly. There are a lot of crescendos in this piece and I would advise not to get too loud too quickly. Here I have inserted some dynamic markings to help you with this. In measure 21 when you return to the *tempo primo*, make sure you get to the right tempo. Don't play slower simply because you've got a beautiful melody to play. Be careful not to accent the first note after the bar line. At measure 53, don't force the tone but use your most beautiful singing and projecting sound.

III. Pan and the Nymphs
This is the most demanding and difficult of all the three movements. When you see a crescendo, don't begin straight away to get loud, but delay the crescendo. I would recommend that you practice your chromatic scales as this will help you play most of this piece. The passage between measures 24-47 can be more successful if you don't try to play too loud. *Staccato*, especially in the low notes, is more successful when you play soft.

I hope you enjoy playing this piece and working on it as much as I have done in the past.

Sir James Galway
Switzerland, 2017

à L. Lafleurance

La Flûte de Pan
Concerto/Sonata for Flute and Orchestra/Piano

I. Pan et les bergers
I. Pan and the Shepherds

Flute

Jules Mouquet, Op. 15
edited by Sir James Galway

O Pan qui habites la montagne, chante nous
de tes douces lèvres une chanson, chante nous
la en t'accompagnant du roseau pastoral.

(Alcée)

4

Flute

Flute

Flute
II. Pan et les oiseaux
II. Pan and the Birds

Assis à l'ombre de ce bois solitaire
ô Pan, pourquoi tires tu de ta flûte ces
sons délicieux?

Flute

Flute

III. Pan et les nymphes

III. Pan and the Nymphs

Silence, grotte ombragée de chênes! Silence, fontaines qui jaillissez du rocher!
Silence, brebis qui bêlez près de vos petits! Pan lui même sur sa flûte harmonieuse
chante, ayant mis ses lèvres humides sur ses pipeaux assemblés. Autour de lui
d'un pied léger, dansent en choeur les Nymphes des eaux et les Nymphes des bois.

(Platon)

Flute

Digital and photographic copying of this page is illegal.

Flute

Flute

12

Flute

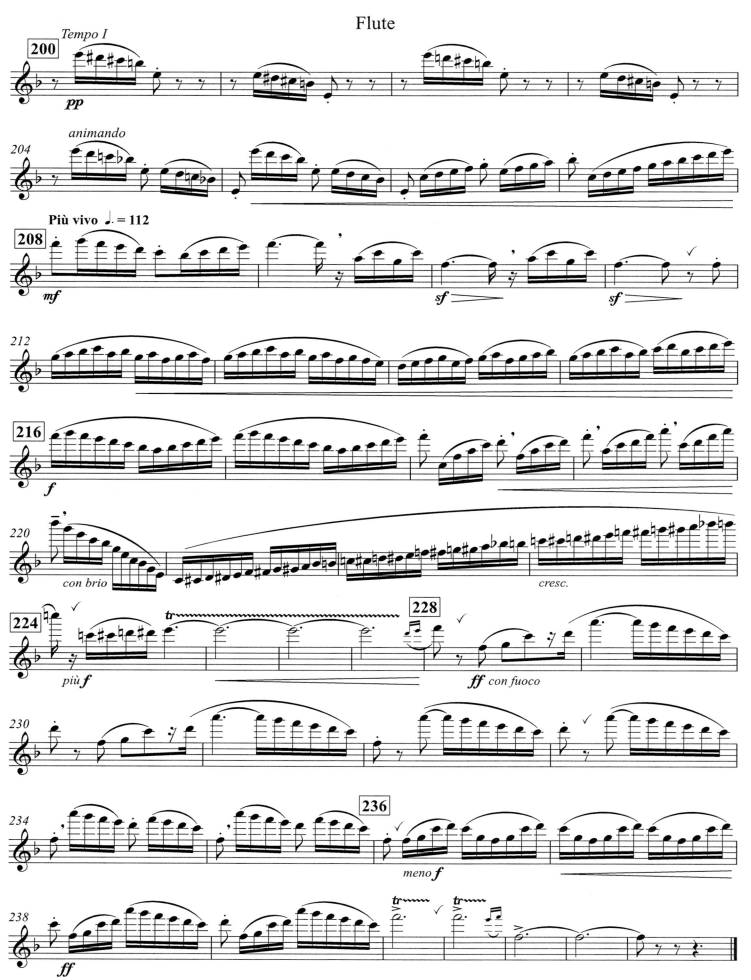

III. Pan et les nymphes
III. Pan and the Nymphs

Silence, grotte ombragée de chênes! Silence, fontaines qui jaillissez du rocher!
Silence, brebis qui bêlez près de vos petits! Pan lui même sur sa flûte harmonieuse
chante, ayant mis ses lèvres humides sur ses pipeaux assemblés. Autour de lui
d'un pied léger, dansent en choeur les Nymphes des eaux et les Nymphes des bois.

(Platon)

Piano